FU YOU TONGUE
HEAVY LAKKA 56

FU YOU TONGUE
HEAVY LAKKA 56

2 Brodah
Josh
En joy these words

IYABA IBO MANDINGO

ISBN: 1533258961
ISBN 13: 9781533258960

iYABARTS, LLC
261 Ely Ave. B15-3F
Norwalk, CT 06854
www.iyabarts.com

Cover Art: "stop n frisk" by Iyaba Ibo Mandingo
Cover Design: Shanna T. Melton/PoeticSoulArts

For my sister Nikki,

Your strength is mine and my strength is yours.

FOREWORD

My first encounter with Iyaba Ibo Mandingo was when I saw a video clip of him on YouTube. Before I could even pay attention to and adequately understand his poetry, his way of rendering it moved me. The facial expression and the body movement spoke very high of the passion that drives him. Here was a performer who was giving all that he had to making the rendition work. He was in the poem and the poem lived through him.

I then paid attention to his verse. Iyaba Ibo Mandingo is a black man, to start with. His poetry is founded not only on his talent as a word artist, but on the honesty of blackness. The honesty of black art is the expression of black pain, of the history of colonialism and slavery that refuses to stay in the past and arrogantly makes its way into the present, of the inevitable and justifiable black rage, of childlike black fears and dreams that have only a slight chance of getting realized.

In "Black woman" he pays homage to the woman who "shines orange yellow like tomorrow sun" and whose "voice is stifled by tradition". This is a woman who stands all kinds of weather and remains intact like a boulder on which nations are standing. But it is also the uncomfortable truth in the poem that makes it a masterpiece: "pussing at the core/ whores to a dick-tionary definition/ stuck in the reflection of a phallic philosophy". This woman is also defined by the same men that she gives birth to and carries on her "broad shoulders" – and remember that the one who defines derives a benefit from the definition.

Mandingo took his first trip to Afrika, the Mother Continent, early in 2015. While a tourist would gaze at the blue sky and admire the landscape, Mandingo connected with his people. He listened to them, embraced them and got embraced by them, he sang and danced with them and allowed himself to cry with them because the pain is the same. He cussed Cecil John Rhodes and his colonial dreams.

In "Poverty of hope" he lets the reader see Johannesburg, once called the City of Gold because of the hope of a better life it symbolized, for what it can really be – a warehouse of hopes and dreams. "they drags bags/ thru the streets of JoBurg/ recycln the city/ stuck in a circle of poverty/ smile thru the struggle for dignity". He laments the "paycheck to paycheck thin line" that characterizes so many a life in Johannesburg.

Mandingo writes in English. It is his means of communication. But the way he massacres and rearranges this English gives one a sense of his love-hate relationship with it. It is like hating a gun because it was used to kill your kith and kin, yet take it because without it there is no way out of the plantation. His language is rooted in his Caribbean roots.

He lives in America and hails from Antigua in the Caribbean islands, but he is Afrikan to the core. And this is because his motherland, Antigua, is as African as Kenya and Ghana. His verse screams and smells Afrika! His issues are the issues of the downtrodden in Accra, Harare, Lagos, Nairobi, Kingston, London,

Berlin, Harlem, Soweto. Through his work one does realize that Afrika is not just the geographical mainland; it is the history and the spirit of her people wherever they are. The Afrika of Iyaba Ibo Mandingo is universal. Our Afrika and our Mandingo is universal.

Mandingo is as mad as the Zimbabwean writer Dambudzo Marechera. It is actually an honour to be mentioned alongside Marechera. But if he stays on his current path, he deserves to be mentioned alongside this luminary. He is on a rampage yet he builds. He dresses the wounds and calls the ghost by their real names.

This is an important volume. It is as much a cry for freedom as it is a celebration of being. Congratulations, Afrikan brother on giving the world this volume.

Sabata-mpho Mokae
Sol Plaatje University
Kimberley, South Africa
August, 2015

INTRODUCTION

I love the way Black people take the English language and turned it into our own thing. "Fu You Tongue Heavy Lakka 56" is Antiguan patios, it's the one thing everyone who knew my Great Grand Mother Rosemond "Rozzy" Guy remembers about her; it was her favorite saying. It means you had a lot to say.

As the grandchild of former enslaved Africans she remembers the elders talking about the heavy plows they used during slavery and the days of shooting hard labor (sharecropping) that followed. The sizes of these plows was designated by a number stamped on the handle, 56 was the number of the heaviest of them all.

For me it was a perfect way to honor my Eguns (ancestors) and the perfect title for a collection of poetry. When the poems started coming; I realized it was also the perfect way to celebrate my native tongue.

The revelation to write in my native patois came in the depths of a writer's block I thought would never go away after def poetry and the "slam thing" made me reevaluate my embracing of this "spoken word" scene.

It was reading the work of African Poets like Don Matterra and Pitika Ntuli that started me contemplating writing in my own language. The experiment was a wonderful revelation of freedom and comfortableness with the syntax that free my imagination to write the words in the same way they were conjugating in my head instead of translating them to American English as I had grown so accustomed to doing.

Iyaba Ibo Mandingo

AFRAID(1ST POEM I EVER WROTE, IOWA JAIL 1989)

Don't be afraid of me becuz I'm black
I don't deserve ur ruthless attack
All I want is to live in peace
But you won't rest until I'm deceased
You brought me here
I never asked to come
Now you tell me go back where I'm from
Are you afraid that I'll do the same
Now that I'm unto ur evil game
Don't blame me, you taught me hate
And now in my eyes you can see ur fate
Ur sins un-repented
Ur debts go unpaid
Don't you think I'm the one
Who should be afraid?

MOMMY ME NO WAN GO MERRICA

Mommi, me no wan go a merrica
nuttin no merry bout merrica
me no wan buy no mango
de a supa market
me wan fu pick um offa mango tree
and besides all the milk and honey
done share out
It's only hand to mouth livin
in government projects
where guns are barking instead of dogs
and sirens replace the crickets and frogs
at night...
the policeman keeps watching me
I see him creeping through my dreams
arresting my aspirations
so Mommi
me no wan go a merrica
cau nuttin nar go merry bout merrica

HOME VIBES

when I think of home
I think of marbles
winner take all and arguments over
whether the winner take all rule
was in effect
kite from coconut tree branch stems
and likkle pissah grandmother cloth
fu make kite tail and string fu fly the kite
we would run and fly kite all day
thru broke up glass bokkle and kassi
and hot asphalt that make you hop like Masai
climbing mango trees and nyamming mango
til the juice run down you arm
and drip off ya elbow
and guava trees
and guava cheese
and bread and cheese
and bun and cheese
and coconut tart that
make ya heart
jump fu carnival
jump fu j'ouvert morning
winding behind some sexy body ghal
running from John Bull…
running from Moco Jumbi
running to play all day in the turquoise ocean
and eat purple beach grapes…

and red juicy pomegranates...
and yellow june plums...
and sweet sap...
and sour sap...
grandmudah woulda mek you eat de stem a de soursop
if you pee pee de bed
fu make you stop pee pee de bed
and cover up under blanket wid soursop leaf bring down fever
rain falling on galvanized roofs
that lull lovers to bed
and children to sleep
to awake to the cockadoodle doo of the cock fowl at dawn
and run and play all day
and remember the joy
of a 3rd world boy
oblivious to the USA

BREBRITCH

Me kcan memba
when we neva hab
no kool aid fu flavor
allwe water...
like J.J Evans inna
no good times ghetto...
smiln good times smile
allwe just drink BreBritch!
suga wata...
so we kcan memba
we come from
captured Afrikans
who pick suga cane
so dat England
& France
& Amsterdam
& Portugal
& Spain
& Merrica
coulda sweeten dem tea!

THE STATUE OF LIBERTY

maybe I blinked but I don't think...
I remember seeing her from the plane
I was looking for an Ellis island vibration
when I entered this nation...
But this place wasn't mine to have...

one day I went looking for her...
to get some liberty from her...
I wondered if she'd have anything to say...
I think they closed her mouth the same day...
they closed Ellis island...

I walked inside her dress
And looked up past her breast...
to see her crown...
here from the ground...

the stairway to her brain moved slowly...
like a midday train...
as I climbed to her top...
the stairwell grew much steeper...
and when I looked the way I came...
the bottom seemed much deeper...

the top was claustrophobic
and made plenty people sick...
the door to the heaven stretched arm was off limits...

no one could go there anymore...
since Ellis island closed her doors...

I wanted to go up there to see...
what Kilpatrick & Goldstein & Carluchi & Smith...see...
But my name is Mandingo
and today it's off limits to me...

She represents america
in more ways than they know...
I climbed to the top to find doors
I could not enter...
Where many did before...but now not anymore...
I descended her stairwell of iron cold...
Realizing miss liberty had lost her soul...
and all her liberty had been sold...
2 those who could pay with their white skin...
Mr. Ellis would check them in...

European second home...
where Indians and buffalo used to roam...
and third world people get sent back home...
by xenophobic offspring
of European boat people
who now write laws...
that would have sent their great grandparents back...
back to Ireland...
back to Italy...
back to Western Europe...
back to feeling black like third world people...
waiting for Mr. Ellis to write his sequel...

from her beacon hand glows worldwide freedom...
cries she with silent lips...
give me your tired your poor...
your huddled masses
yearning to breathe free
I lift my lamp beside the golden door...
but for third world people
there doesn't seem to be a
knob anymore
So maybe
I blinked...

ANCESTORS

He sits to me like a tired old warrior
Contemplatn his youth
Of battles lost n won
And of his search for truth
Imagining myself as him and traveling
back in time to see America
in technicolored black n white...
when ku klux klan burned crosses in the night
and response to our black demands were mute
and southern magnolia bore dead castrated peculiar fruit
when jim crow signs showed us our water fountains
and before Martin Luther climbed his mountains
thru all of this and countless more
walked this old man who sits next door
with skin so full of melanin
the south must have been rough for him
he must've swallowed all his pride
to take america in stride
and still be here at 96
in spite of all the sticks and stones
they used to try and break our bones
and hoovers taps on Huey phones
and all the blood that spill and run
from US manufactured guns
thru all the lying presidents
and all the time they raised the rent
and all the blacks to war they sent

to die for them...
and all the sellout niggers who lie for them
thru all of this this old man walked
and still to hear him talk
his strength remains
his pride remains
his love remains
his stride; it remains
he died this year but I will not forget
and I haven't forgotten you Mother dear
the wailing of your cries
it lives within my ears
I haven't forgotten the way they held you down
upon the ground...
so each could have a turn
ripping your dress
stealing your pureness...
I haven't forgotten the way it felt to only have your child for a while
And fear the auctioneer
Becoming human steer...
I remember your Womanhood
You could pick 50 satchels of cotton
I haven't forgotten
You could face the whip
three months within a ship
founding fathers invading hips...
Stealing your sons and daughters away
Today Afrikan names become smith
And black people seem to love it
And are willing to sit
And watch them...

Colonize you
Imperialize you
And tarzan movie trivialize you
But the warmness of your tropical womb
I still remember
Sucking raw melanin from your breast
Mount Kilimanjaro peaks
My cheekbones
Black skin nose and lips
Survive the ships
And whips
And founding fathers invading hips
So they see your faces today too
I'll make them remember
What they did to you!

TREES

Yesterday a tree spoke to me
in Mississippi
she beckoned me to her softly
wanting no one to hear her horrid tales
of bearing strange fruit
her truth
she'd always try to hide
behind the other trees
by pulling in her limbs and leaves
when they came
but that never made them leave her alone
Instead she'd moan
as they dragged another screaming
body to her trunk
bending over she showed me the limb
they would choose
to hang the noose
and cried a sticky sap
as she placed the tortured limb into my lap
so I could see the gash left in her skin
from being abused again and again
to lynch black men
and sticky sap dripped on my face
as she recalled the horrifying screams
that haunted her dreams
at night
and how the victims fought

the choking rope
choking hope away with hate
suffocating future dreams
asphyxiating life away
with tarred and feathered flames
and sticky sap dripped on my face
as she recalled the smell of chewing tobacco
and gasoline
and fear
and hatred
and burning flesh
and laughter
mocking laughter
inhuman indifferent laughter
that floated up to her upper limbs
blocking them from the sun
causing her leaves to wither and fall
to the ground
where her roots moaned in guilty agony
see, she felt guilty...
guilty for being an accomplice
to murder and torture
and now sticky sap poured from every pore of that tree
onto me
and I had to hug that tree
so she could see
that their hate was never hers in my eyes
I never blamed you for the hate of savages
who used your limbs to perpetrate their cowardice
I never blamed you
we never blamed you

they never blamed you
those brothers and sisters who swung
from your limbs
so don't cry my sister tree
we know the fear and share the agony
of not knowing when
or how
to run
from this
amerikkkan
hate

41 TIMES

It takes 41 bullets to quiet ur fears
41 times for ur goosebump hairs
41 times I grew in ur eyes
41 times to shrink me to size
41 times u thought u saw a gun
41 times I didn't try to run
41 times and big mouth rudy still can say
41 times a grand jury should lead the way
41 times and you still get paid leave
41 times my mother will have to grieve
41 spheres of ur fear u hurled at me
41 times my black skin was all you could see
41 times to make you feel brave
41 times I was a revenging slave
41 times some lynch mob from ur past
Move like a spirit possessing ur ass
41 times you pulled out your rope
41 times to strangle my throat
41 times to make u feel calm
41 times and I was never armed
41 times for this racial schism to grow still more
41 times more black blood spilled out on the floor

So yesterday...yesterday I ordered
3 bulletproof vest
I have 3 boys to past ur test
That's 3 boys with melanin

In their skin
So I'm teaching them bout reaching
For anything round their waist
Cause I know u won't waste time
Stealing their lives from me
I'm letting them know
How to turn round reallllllllllllllllllllllllllllllllll
Slow…so you can know it's not a gun you see
And send them home alive to me
I'm teaching them how to duck
In case you try their luck
Duck boy duck
Duck roll and run some more
I won't let them outside the door of my eyes view
I pray to be with them when they run into u
I'm jumping outta bed
With visions in my head
Of dead phone calls
And standing in dark halls
At the morgue
With one million mothers crying
Dressed in their best black dress
Wishing they'd ordered
my bulletproof vest
over protective and paranoid too
but all I can do
is all I can do
to keep my 3 sons safe from you
I'll make them allergic to 5-0 blue
What's else can I do
I have 3 Amadous?

9-11

I wonder if I'll be ostracized and criticized
By all you americans in this room
If I say the chickens
have come home to roost
As you throw up your bloody hands
Why me?
What have I done?
And now
Your city's shitty streets
Look like downtown Vietnam
And Beirut and the Congo
And Palestine and Burundi
And Rwanda and Grenada
And Panama
And Baghdad
And you're throwing up your bloody hands
Lamenting over your plight
Of domestic flights flying into famous skylines
Destroying famous landmarks
Destroyed
Like the hopes of the people in the Congo
When you replaced Lumumba with Mobutu
Destroyed
Destroyed like the hope of the people in Chile
When you replaced Allende with Pinochet
Destroyed
Destroyed like the hope of the people in Jamaica

When you replaced Manley with Seaga
Destroyed
Destroyed like the hope of African Americans
When you replaced Malik with Jesse
Destroyed
Destroyed like Soweto and Biko
Destroyed
Destroyed like Kenya and Jomo
Destroyed
Destroyed like your national security as
Innocent Americans die wondering why
They're not safe anymore
See, reciprocity comes boomeranging back
Bringing with it the smell of death
From Vietnam and Iraq and Nagasaki
And repercussions for the years and years
Of hegemony as the memories of Japanese
Kamikazes shining like pearl harbors
Hijack American security
Hijack American superiority
Hijack American Democracy
To be spun into yellow journalism accusations
And speculations bout whodunit
But the chickens have come home to roost
Now all you want to do is throw up your bloody hands
And they are bloody up to your wrists
Up to your forearms
Up to your elbows
Up to your armpits
Up to your shoulders
Up to your neck

Up to the level of vengeance sometimes
And yes, innocent people die sometimes
Like 1 million dying in 100 days in Rwanda
While you all changed the channel
To congressional executive decision
To replace and assassinate
3rd world heads of state
Trying to decide our own fate
As African Americans
wrapped themselves in the flag
Born again patriots who forget that same flag
Flew over Jefferson's Monticello
while he capitalized
On captured African lives
Creating American capitalism
The center of your foreign policy
And I see you watching me in my beard scared
Wondering could I be Osama
Coming home with my chickens
On this plane filled with drama?

KATRINA

Backstroking through New Orleans
Smelling death and hopelessness on
Every breath
Rest is not an option
A father let his wife slip away
To save their kids today
Live on CNN in water
up to his chest
on a street he used to walk
Looking for a job
In a city ignoring
Black men and their problems
Long before a hurricane came to shed light
On his plight
in a country still trying to figure
how to stop saying nigga to 3rd world
Homemade refugees
Calling the superdome home; but

"home is where the hatred is, home is filled with pain...
and it might not be such a bad idea
if they neva, if they neva
went home again" (Gil Scott Heron)

Stand as far away from me as you can
and tell me you understand
My blues
Newsflash, most of the people in the flood
Have Africa in their blood
And already knew
George Bush wouldn't stop his vacation
to visit no 3rd world US Nation
Of homemade Refugees
his momma can't see
unless they're serving her tea
So go ahead
swallow that bitter bush
Stuff the hemlock down your throat
Remember you voted
for this motherfucker
Who never gave a fuck
bout all them black mothers
Hanging from rooftops
up to their chest in the reality of life
In America...
when your skin has melanin
& Helicopters won't land
& The president won't hold your hand
And nobody...
nobody will give a damn!

AMERIKKKAN EXILE...

Sometimes the caged door feels closer
than my skin
Close enough to interrupt the rhythm
of my breathing
And now I'm vomiting up the lies I've told myself
To remain a Babylonian
A citizen of a doomed society
who won't see the writing on the walls
All super power nations fall
Rome's fate awaits
the kingdom of george washington
george bush will push the final straws
of vengeance
Into the fires of vengeance
bringing vengeance home to rest
And I wanna get out
wanna run like Lot
to a plot of land not soaking with blood
And suffering in the name Of Babylon...
where people can
Look me in the face and say Ase O
and mean it from their soul
So I can feel that love vibe
and replenish my soul
Gone cold to feed the flesh
This shit is getting thick
Thick enough to stifle hope

so I smoke marijuana
To keep it all at bay
till I can get away to that place in my head
Where people ain't dead
from manmade bullets flying
and politicians lying
Taking other people shit
and not paying them for it
Sucking 3rd world blood
through rose colored straws
Hiding behind laws
meant to cloak their true intentions
…contented Babylonians sit
and watch a world die
And no one cried
till Babels tower fell
and broke
the spell
That all was well
So I plot like Lot to get out one night soon
For yonder darkness looms

THE GREATEST DEPRESSION

2 watch a giant fall
I stood against a wall
and felt the street
crumble unda my feet
defeat
comes slooooooow when
at one's own hand
command of self-control
rolls slowly
down
a
growing
deficit...
C.E.O's
avoid
the
shit with parachutes
that open into
million dollar
severance
checks...checks and balances
stop balancing since profit
became the means to an end
ending corporate allegiance 2 the state faith in a dollar bill
lobbyist can rent a politician's will
I've lost my will 2 care
standing here with my back against this wall

begging on this naked street
pocket fulla holes...
holding on 2 a dream of america
my mother carried tucked inside her hopes 4 a betta life
on our illegal migration 2 this nation
but smoke gets in your eyes
when you try looking around illusions
2 make ends meet

RICHARD PRYOR

laughing
splitting sides
bent over in pain...
belly tightens
turning inside out...
drooling out of mouth...
insight too honest to avoid...
Freud's id
in techn-colored man
doing black humor...
wid a black fist
2 a white crowd...laughing out loud...
at themselves
2 avoid hearing accusations smuggled in2 punch lines...
making laugh lines
ache with revelations...
of a nation suppressing
the joyous nature of a people...
inclined to laugh
at life's misfortunes...
instead of crying...
laughing...
instead of dying...
living...
through amos & andy points of view...
you tore off the mask...caste in the days...
of black face and yes-sar bossing

tossing it in2 yesterday's notion
of what a Black man is...
changing with the times...
living through the fire...with a smile...
all the while...
laughing at the pain...
laughing at yourself...
instead of lying 2 yourself...
instead of lying 2 us...
instead of lying 2 them...
bout everything it takes
to make it through a day...
as a Black man...
in a land...
that everyday...
in so many ways...
make it so mutha fuckin
hard 2 smile...

GLOBAL WARMING 1

a wind blew in from the north
with truth on her lips...
ships float thru the poles
with no more ice to hold their hulls in place...
chasing dead polar bears floating south
with tomorrow in their mouth...
...repercussions falling back to earth
thru broken ozone...layers
praying neva made more sense than now...
watch'n cherry blossoms bloom in winter...
winter in july?
a sunny december sky...
the weather man just lied again...
2morrow it could rain...
or sleet...
or snow...
...who knows?!
who knew penguins flew...?
but what else can they do?
with the ground under their feet melting slowly everyday...
maybe...perhaps...
perhaps we don't need the polar caps...
polar bears can sip ice water
as they float down stream
in2
extinction

GLOBAL WARMING 2[MYCHU]

I met an Eskimo
in Hawaii...
said he was doing
research...

GOLIATH & DAVID (4 PALESTINE)

1 rock...
from a hand...flung against
a tank...destroying childhood
memories...

2 rocks...
from a hand...thrown
against a wall...built
with bricks of hate...

3 rocks
from a hand...thrown
against missiles with
P.L.O DNA detection
sensors made in the USA
fastened to their noses...

4 rocks...
from a hand...flung against
hovering helicopters...anxious
to kill a hundred innocents
to get one guilty of standing
up 2 straight...

5 rocks...
in Goliath's Hand
David will not share the
land...
so now Goliath stands alone
on battlefield
with sling and stone...

AYITI

I feel you Haiti
Feel you like the
spine running
down my back...
taste the neglect of a
Western world still
scorning you...
for birthing
Toussaint...Dessalines...
for ripping Napoleon's
shackles from your
soul...
from being swallowed
whole...by a greedy
France...
your circumstance
has never been
by chance
you were singled out...
for erecting a Black
Republic...
in the land of the
white man...
paying for your
freedom with a debt of
poverty...
stuck at the wrong end of a Christian

nose looking down at
you...
scared a your voodoo
send Dambala
to take pat robertson's eyes
so he can see his
own lies...
woven into a way of life
that eats the strife
of third world labor
see the Bauxite
America stole
like Montezuma's gold...
Hold on a little longer
if you can...
I see your hand
reaching through
the rubble
of your country's trouble...

55 MYKUS

Written during the 55 days with Homeland Security for my poem 9-11.

Day 1)   You'll only know
          you're in a police state
          when they come 4 you...

Day 2)   handcuffs feel like
          manacles...
          feels like my ancestors
          wrist...
          I remember this...

Day 3)   The black ink
          stole my fingerprints...
          the flash bulb
          stole my face...

Day 4)   bend over...spread ur
          cheeks...and cough...
          cough out your manhood &
          then try to stand up!

Day 5)   2 white shirt...
          2 white draws...
          2 white socks...
          2 many fucking locks!

Day 6)   The plastic plexiglass
              window
              takes the warmth
              from the sunlite...

Day 7)   If I inhale deeply
              I can fill this cell
              with me...

Day 8)   Eating in here is a chore...
              cellie take the rest
              I don't want no more!

Day 9)   My head space
              & this dirty ass
              cot...
              is all I got...

Day 10)   This c.o. looks like
              Justin volpe
              And that's his last name too...
              shit...somebody
              hide all the broomsticks!

Day 11)   Yesterday I watched a
              Butterfly fly...
              really fly...for the
              1st time...

Day 12)   The butterfly came back today
           teasing me...flying in & out
           of the razor wire on top
           the fence...
           I hate dat...fucking...butterfly...

Day 13)   this place seeps into you
           like cold slow death...
           I haven't smiled in 13 days!

Day 14)   my face feels
           stuck in this contorted
           scowl...
           this cave man body
           language...

Day 15)   I know why the
           caged bird cries...
           and why the caged bird dies...

Day 16)   I read anything that
           takes my mind away
           from these
           4 walls and this shrinking
           plastic window...

Day 17)   a handful of
           potato chips...
           eat like a jar
           of caviar behind bars...

Day 18)   my cellie lives here!
             once in a while...
             he goes
             home
             for a vacation...

Day 19)   this place seeps into you
             slowly
             the monotony
             is killing me

Day 20)   this morning I had
             2 slices of white bread...
             2 swallows of orange juice...
             & eggs yellow number
             six...

Day 21)   I did a drawing
             of Jesus
             for a package of
             tuna & 2 soups...

Day 22)   in here wealth is
             determined
             by the size of
             your commissary...
             and I don't have any...

Day 23)   jail is like the ghetto
             with the volume
             turned all the
             way up...

Day 24)   men who are told
            what to do...
            by men who are told what to do...
            I gotta get outta
            here...

Day 25)   I watched a camera
            watch me wipe
            my ass today...

Day 26)   Only the awake
            time counts...so I
            sleep a lot...

Day 27)   the butterfly came
            back 2day...
            I'm jealous of her wings...

Day 28)   16 hr shift for 20 years
            C.O. do time too...
            Locked up with me and you!

Day 29)   visitors equal cavity
            search...
            mommy please don't
            visit...

Day 30)   talking through glass...
            all the words bounce back at
            you...

Day 31)   The doors in
            here echo
            when they slam

Day 32)   metals bouncing
            off metal...
            blending with the wailing
            of lonely men...

Day 33)   the phone here gets
            more loving than a
            5 dollar whore!

Day 34)   baby I love you!
            baby when I come
            home...
            I'll never leave you
            again...

Day 35)   I cooked tuna
            & Ramen noodles
            in a plastic bag...
            4 dinner

Day 36)   I ain't got
            no time...
            to do time...
            so I'm done wasting mine...

Day 37)   I can taste my
           woman...on the
           wall next to my bed...

Day 38)   I gave my hand
           my woman's
           name...
           and stayed in bed
           an extra hour...

Day 39)   dese niggas in
           here r upset...
           cuz they ain't
           got no pussy
           to pet!

Day 40)   men in boxes...
           with locks...
           and hard cocks
           the tension smells
           like RAPE...

Day 41)   at first you
           dread...all the alone
           time...
           inside your head

Day 42)   waiting to be exiled
           I take Buddha
           breaths...
           to stretch...my
           patience...
           I cannot let them
           see me cry...

Day 43)   I wear my manhood
           in the screw face
           I carry everyday...
           what you looking at
           nigga?
           get outta my way!

Day 44)   the butterfly came
           back again today...
           I refused to speak
           to her...
           I think she was laughn
           at me...

Day 45)   I'm beginning
           to hate things...
           with wings...

Day 46)   the lawyer
            came today...
            said that there
            might be a way...
            I listen with one ear...
            hope in here...
            is death...

Day 47)   I wrote
            to a man's
            wife a pagefull of prose
            and told her
            how good she
            smelled with
            his nose...
            cuz he was 35...
            and couldn't spell his own
            jive

Day 48)   damn I miss
            my woman...
            miss her soft
            curves...
            with all these
            hard muthafuckas
            everywhere...

Day 49)   The lawyer
            spoke to my wife today
            told her there
            might be a way
            I smiled thru the
            phone at her "good" news...

Day 50)   comradery is a
            necessity
            in here
            somebody gotta
            watch your rear...

Day 51)   2 nite makes
            51 nites and days...
            the warden says
            the government pays...
            double to house
            immigration cases...
            double!

Day 52)   the lawyer
            doesn't realize
            his good news
            is not worth
            the cavity search...
            just get me the
            fuck out!

Day 53)   hope got me choking on the rage
                 pacing back
                 & forth in my
                 cage

Day 54)   I was supposed
                 to go to court today...
                 hope had my wife
                 & mother crying
                 all the way home
                 without me...
                 fuck hope!

Day 55)   C.O woke me up
                 with a tap on
                 my cot...
                 and told me pack up
                 all the shit
                 I got...

WOMAN

She left the taste of purple
on my tongue
there where bitter and sweet
meet
And now
I feel her every time
I swallow!

CRAVE

when u crave her
hard enuf to taste
the arch in her spine
on the tip of ur
mind clear as the moment
u knew
she would own
a space in u
4ever...heard
in the braille of a scream
in a moment of absolute trust
carnal lust
gainst the rhythm of
a stroke...gainst the rhythm of a wantn
hot as an equator morning
sweat gainst the taunt of flesh
sweet gainst the want of flesh
clear as the moment...
you knew
you would
crave her
4 always

CHALICE

Congregatn inna
1ness
sitn crossd leg
b4 a Nyabinghi flame
to give Izes
in the name of
JAH RASTAFARI
lift tam offa locks
and sip chalice cup
inhaln peace
exhaln confusion
herb is the healn of the nation

RELIGION

a chu you no know
Odu a come outta cowrie shell
Long before dem invent
heaven n hell
& bible spell
fu quell you Black intentions

PO TANG POKO TANG

ether bound
watching ground become irrelevant
meditation ancient
ebony hands make congo drums
hummm
binary code in patois
wha mek we dey ya
wha mek we dey ya
po tang poko tang!
po tang poko tang!

MORNING SPLIFF

early morning dew
collects on blade of grass
falsetto yellow breast
seduces mate
from mango tree perch
nectar filln nostrils
cottony cumulus clouds
drift open
tangerine sunshine wakes
epidermis
bright and ready
for the day
ganja exhale

BROTHER

allwe just race up mango tree
and nyam mango plenty
allwe just catch guppy deh a country pond
and fry dem down wid unyan
allwe fly kite
and ride bike
and say rasshole and skunt and
rassclart and fuck
when no big people round
allwe get blow fu cuss badwud
when big people round
and go market go buy coal
allwe just laaf arffa people n church
and run from johnbull
and run go see de Moco Jumbi
and run past de obeah man house
dem say he just cook darg and so in dey
and me just push you near he gate
and you just friken
and say 'me go tell pan you rasshole!'
when no big people round
except fu de time ms joseph hear me a cuss
and say 'ya bouye me go tell you grandy whey you out ya a say!'
and muddah bang allwe fu cus badwud in fronta big people...
and allwe just laugh plenty
and fart plenty
and fight ova denise fu joe from next doe...plenty

and allwe peep inna ms minny doe
and allwe get catch and get more blow
and allwe hold hand de a mudah funeral
and hold hand come a merrica
allwe build snow man
and allwe nyam pizza
allwe talk bout ghal
and play baseball
and play football
and you just say 'but a how dem call dis football when you nar use
you foot and call football soccer?'
and allwe talk bout life
and start mek choice
and start do wrong
allwe go allwe separate way
allwe tun drug dealer
allwe tek one life
allwe get 35 years
and allwe still a try
and thinkn bout allwe
just mek allwe cry.

THE POET

Thru de long eyelash
that can see jumbi
me a watchu
swallow my antiquities
n turn dem inna tourist attraction
diamonds on ur breath
u reek of genocide
planetary rapist
hidn behind a racism
that traps the world in black n white
when 3quarter of the planet is colord
Elegba eyes see you
whispering bible into African ears
jesus on ur breath
you reek of contradiction
benedictions from pedophile
on their knees
"1st" world
implodn softly
like dandelions petals on the wind
written down
in paint and pen

MUDDAH(GRANDMOTHER)

that last rain puddle
sent me back thirty-eight years
holding muddah hand

MUDDAH DOCUNA, CHOPCHOP &SALTFISH RECIPE

fuss you haffu
grate coconut
n grate sweet potato
mix in
cinnamon
and nutmeg
and likkle essense
wid likkle wata
and stir um
stir um til ebryting mix in
and trow in likkle flour
mix um up propaly
til you hab one nice batta
and den get some banana leaf
pour in de batta
and wrap dem up nice
use likkle strip offa de leaf
fu tie um off
and drop dem inna

one pot a boiln wata
while dem a boil
peel and cut up two eggplant
and boil um wid some okra and fresh spinach...
when dem done boil
drain off de wata
and mix in likkle butta
and some black peppa
and chop um up good
til all a dem mix up
when dat done
tek you saltfish
mek sure you boil um couple time
so some a de salt will come off
stew down some
onion
and green peppa
and scotchbonnet
inna likkle oil
and likkle tomato paste
inna one frying pan
and den add in the saltfish
strip um up likkle bit;
but not too much
cova um and mek um
boil out likkle bit
when it ready
just tek the docuna outta de leaf
and set um inna de plate
some people ago warn two
cau you know dem lub you muddah docuna

tek some a de chopchop
and put um pan de plate
and tek de stew down saltfish
and put um pan tap a de chopchop
allyou ready fu gynam?
yes muddah!

KALI

Kali tree blooming
rastaman meditating
on the fruits to come

HER

she stands tall and strong
like a tree in the forest
of my existence

DE SWEETEST MANGO

mango look ready
catch de fruit bfore ee drop
sexy island ghal

MUSIC WOMAN

she grinds hard and slow
music flowing from her hips
calypso woman

4 RICHIE HAVENS(N ODE)

a poet
became his words 2day
love warrior
truth totn troubadour
priestly precepts on guitar string
pluckn and pulln
pluckn and pulln
town cryn woodstock rebel
baritone griot
wrapn freedom in love songs
to a country n a ppl
still tryna be
their/its betta self
pluckn and pulln
pluckn and pulln
truth from guitar string
and a baritone mouth that moan the hopes

of ur generation
n my generation
n those generations
2 come

A DAMEK

suga wata memories
we run barefoot
thru broke up glass bokkle
kassie and hot asphalt
shoes a fu skool and chuch
dutty foot battom fulla nail dig
and coal bun
haffu wash off before
allwe go inside a night time else
muddah will box off you ear n dem
and ask you if you def
learn trade wid
grandfadah
inna tailor shop
a mek suit and form de ass
and drink Antigua cavalier rum
and watch de woman and dem pass
from behind
a damek me lub watch
woman battom so much

a damek me just wax nostalgic so much
a damek
a damek me lub drink
suga wata so much
a damek
ee just mek me memba
whey me come from
a damek

HOME SICK

missing Wadadli
longn to sit down unda
a shady tree
and feel my grandmuddah's
voice in the breeze
hear my grandfadah's laugh
in the crash of waves
south where the fisherman patriarch
come from
east where mudah people dem
come from
barefoot in the soil
feeln generations

THIS POEM

an earful
an eyeful
crawl up skin on goosebump hairs
chill down spine
nourish a famishd heart
summer smile on winter day
lover's plea of yellow words
4 bright blue sex
that reeks of her in spring time bloom
a father's love
a mother's hope
man to woman is so unjust
woman to man is so unjust
rhyming every line
tired of the spoken words
mastrubatn gesticulations
slam slambo slam!
close minded open mics
a secret lover's smile
in the darkness of the light of day
the reckoning...
apology wrapd in lavender loveliness
an ode...
an ode to the muse who inspires these words
a political rant that becomes a manifesto
a dogma an ideology...a fuckn way of life
a reason to swear shit mudah fucka dayum

the angst
the purge
the declaration
the observation
the imitation
the flattery...the flattery my ass!
the journey in 2 get out
of the rat race running on fast food
and soda pop
the black bag the brown man
if you see something...
say something! say something! say something!
it could be a bum-bo clart bomb
embracn native tongue
me go talk how me learn fu talk
and tap worry bout what you tink bout my patois
like a Willy Perdomo stanza
dripn with mufungo
funkn to the rhythm of a line
star gazing thru the cosmos on saturn's rinnnnnngggggggsssss
singn negro spirituals to hide the writer's block
memorizing
reciting
scoring
ignoring
this
poem

4 MAMA ASSATA #1

suffer'n and smil'n
a so dem like we
lip skin pull'd back against teeth
beg'n for tomorrow's bread
head bow'd
but white hot fear
curls up white skin
when mirror liquifies
drown'n clandestine deeds
in karma
when afro'd heads rise
and beg'n hands
become clinch'd fist
resistance internal
resistance external
reflect'n patriotic hate
we will feed our children
we will care for our elders
we will secure our community
we will resist you
bullet for bullet
blood for blood
dogma for dogma
change for change
change for change
we will fight you
until you
change!

4 MAMA ASSATA #2

was wonder'n
how come nobody neva
go after none a dem
white man
stand'n round in dem lynch'n photographs
smiln sunday morning smiles
lov'nly embrac'n their sons
hoist'n dem unto their shoulders
smil'n jesus loves me smiles
guilty of terrorist murder
by "patriot act" definition
where is their million dolla bounty
liv'n free wid no statute of limitation
on kill'n
4 terror's sake
while Black n Brown
prisoners of politricks
sit behind american steel
stolen leadership
guilty of kill'n ur perfect society
where white men
can stand around at lynch'ns
hold'n their sons lov'nly at the shoulders
smil'n sunday morning smiles
into the camera

4 MAMA ASSATA #3

warrior mother
creatn life
in the iron belly
of the beast
we; children
of your conviction
your resistance
shackle breakn woman
power to the people
the struggle continues
you are still our Champion
our light in the distance
warrior queen
fist into the sky
they cannot have you

4 MAMA ASSATA #4

guilty at birth
from color of skin
and pride of memory
Tubman D.N.A
Sojouner D.N.A
Wells D.N.A
Bethune D.N.A
Plantation Healer D.N.A
Midwife pickney bring'n D.N.A
Queen Mother D.N.A
Black and Proud
in spite of whitewash brainwash whitewash brainwash whitewash-
brainwashwhitewashbrainwashwhitewashbrainwash
BLACK!!!
MUTHAFUCKA...
BLACK POWER!!!
is all we need to
wash the white away
from brains stuck on blond
blue eyed beauty
my skin is BLACK
my queen is BLACK
i love BLACK
BLACK fist
BLACK afro
BLACK locks

BLACK LOVE
LOVE BLACK
BLACK LOVE
LOVE BLACK
BLACK
LOVE

4 MAMA ASSATA #5

safe in Cuba's
embrace
protectd by a ppl
that love the Oya in you
warrior elder
revolutionary mother
raise'n us on pride and dignity
nurtur'n us with a love 4 our ppl
sacrific'n everything
so we could be a little freer
in our continental cage
of smoke n mirrors
they still call us niggers behind closed doors
still malign and assume
still profile and consume
still arrest and shoot at will
still target practice
still...
still want your pound of flesh
for their altar of revenge
but we will hold you up
safe in our embrace
warrior elder
because we love the Oya in you

4 MAMA ASSATA #6

Black Woman
backbone to a continent
power of the Nile
beauty of the summer sun
shoulder strong enough to carry hope
strong enough to carry a nation
Harriet gun at the ready
READY!!!
original womb
strength of labor
in iron dungeon
love in an envelope of hate
Black solidarity
I got you and you got me
remaining human
in the throes of inhumanity
stronger than they figured
jersey turnpike assassins
didn't realize Harriet's railroad
stopd in Cuba

4 MAMMA ASSATA #7

I feel your power
in the wind mamma Oya
you more free than we

BLACK LIKE WE

the ital rhythm in our steps
this Black strut...
on display everyday...
Sarkie Baartman dissected...
erect Black penis...
envy...
walkn like an Egyptian thru time
Reminding a 4getful planet...
of the way
BLACK home...
written n2 stubborn chromosomes
translated n2 sanskrit...
and Inca...
and Aztec...
and Adinkra...
Yoruba...Hausa...Ashanti...Bantu...Zulu...
Raped into
english...
falling off of Native tongues...

spokn in electric guitar
spilln out of Blues shamans
creating binary codes in
Rock n Roll...
and Jazz...
and Hip Hop...
teachn an entire planet
our Black strut!

REFLECTIONS (A MYCHU)

my eyes reflect your truths
killing me will not relieve
your guilty conscience

4 TRAYVON MARTIN

GRRRRRRR!!!
Lurkn n the shadows of ur CONSCIENCE...
Ur historical guilt...
U have been KILLN me since the beginning!
Winning favor from ur tribe with TROPHIES of my BONES...
Hidn ur lust 4 BLACK flesh nside...
EMMETT TILL accusations...
I AM YOUR BOOGIE MAN!!!
The OFFSPRING of your DEEDS!
Fed on the HATRED of ur 4fathers...
Growing n2 boomeranging VENGEANCE...
STILL whistling EMMETT TILL...
Still swinging by the neck from the limbs of ur fears!
Still BRANDED with ur CROSSHAIRS...
STILL!!!
BLACK BOY!
Make no sound...
Be STILL...
You were BORN with the bullet of ur existence...
Labeled endanger-ous @ BIRTH...
U will have 2 learn a docile smile...
Hide ur GRRRRR!!!
Behind complacent eyes...
I cannot protect you from the HATE...
Nor the FEAR...
I cry the TEARS of helpless fathers...
Wondering what 2 do...
2 remove the BULLS EYE from you...

4giVe me 4 bringing U n2 THIS world...
christened
BLACK BOY!
Endangered! Dangerous!
Danger!
Following in ur shadows...
So do not pull up ur HOODIE...
Do not GROW 2 be tall...
Do not scare the nice WHITE lady...
Do not go OUTSIDE @ all!!!
Do not stare @ the POLICE man...
Do not ever hide UR hands...
Do not question what I'm sayn...
N do not try 2 OVERSTAND...
Do not GRRRRR!!!
When UR in public...
N do not GRRRRR!!!
When UR @ home...
Do not GRRRRR!!!
With the POLICE man...
Only GRRRRR!!!
When UR alone...
Nside this world I give 2 you...
Inherited from my FATHER...
Inherited from his FATHER...
Inherited from his FATHER...
Inherited from his FATHER...
Inherited from the BLACK AFRIKAN who was broken @ the whip...
Shattered n2 a million pieces of confusion...
So the white man could slumber under his blanket of wickedness...

4 MIKE BROWN

Draped in empty DECLARATIONS!
Hiding weak CONSTITUTIONS!
Pouring poisoned lust n2 raped AFRIKAN bellies...
Running from the BOOGIE MAN u created...
The one who would do 2 u...
What U would do if you had done...
The things you've done...
2 me...
Don't it make U wanna GRRRRRRRRRAB!!!
The nearest WHITE MAN and rip him limb from limb!!!
Force ur FAITH on him!
Force ur NAME on him!
Force ur RACE on him!
Force ur BLAME on him!
So that you can sleep @ night...
Without jumping out of bed in fright...
Wondering if ur SONS will be alright!

4 ERIC GARNER

til blue blood
is as valuable as black blood
red blood will run
and puddle at your feet
feedn nonviolence 2 violence

a moment of silence for innocence
lost 2 long ago 2 remember
when blue gainst black didn't meant red
blood everywhere...
or blood no where at all...
blood everywhere...
or blood no where at all...
blood everywhere...
or blood no where at all...
when the madness boomerangs
when the tables turn
my tears 4 ur tears
my fears 4 ur fears...
my woman cries
ur woman cries
my whys
for your whys
when the assailant says
"i was scared"
"it felt like I was fightn a demon"
a boogieman
dressd in the skin of ur imagination
ur birth of a nation indoctrination
irish flatfoot flogn flesh
passing down the british blight
in a whirlwind of madness
blowing gainst
the fabric of ur convictions
gainst
the fabric of the blue wall of violence
gainst

the fabric of ur
"i can breathe cuz i didn't resist"
T-Shirts

CLOCK TOWER

from the clock tower
downtown amerikkka...
where 2morrow always feel like yesterday
in the blink of n eye
plantation shutterd window opens
curtains flutter
in the southern breeze
inhale magnolia leaves
exhale hanging trees
aiming n waiting
aiming n waiting...
and aiming and waiting...
Blacker than the sum of your fears
boogieman cloaked in revenge conceived
deserved and never received...
Frankenstein runs from his monster
holdn mirror to the horror
of a truth woven into dna
in nursery rhythms and parlor games
aunt jemima uncle ben
i got plenty nigger friends
aunt jemima uncle ben
i got plenty nigger friends

aunt jemima uncle ben
i got plenty nigger friends
aiming n waiting
aiming and waiting
aiming and waiting
funeral dirge for my nigga
we be mo trigga happy than dey be...
trigga happy than dey be...
trigga happy than they be...
longs we shootn at we...
indoctrinated fratricide justifying homicide
got this suicide shooter standing...
in the cradle of this clock tower
strikes eleventh hour
lynchn rope dangln from throat
Amadou Diallo bullet hole leaking
Jordan Davis innocence
boogieman!!!
leaking Patrick Doresmond innocence
boogieman!!!
leaking Oscar Grant innocence
boogieman!!!
leaking Sean Bell innocence
boogieman!!!
leaking Trayvon Martin innocence
boogieman!!!
leaking Micheal Brown innocence
boogieman!!!
leaking Emmett Till innocence
boogieman!!!
waiting and aiming

waiting and aiming
waiting and aiming
and aiming
and aiming
and aiming
and aiming
and aiming
and...

EULOGY(A MYKU)

DIE CRACKA
SO COMPLETELY...
DAT UR CRUMBS
4GET THEIR ORIGIN!

TOWN CRIER 4 BABA GIL NOBEL

SELF KNOWLEDGE!!!
On my TV screen...
In between the avalanche of propaganda...
aimed @ lulln me 2 death...
Steadfast town crier steady N my adolescent ear...
WAKE UP!!!
I met U standn outside Attica's walls...
microphone N hand
staring N2 an ABC camera...

Pain of a revolution yelln from your face...
Ur honest face that said; I LOVE MY PEOPLE!
N u bCame my sunday morning church...
12pm ABC you N me...
N eye met our revolution thru ur eyes...
Sheros N Heros...
Warriors N Martyrs...
Singers N Players of Instruments...
Dancers N Poets...
Writers N Scholars...
Preachers N Politicians...
Artist N Teachers...
N people...
my people...
our people...
In our Joy N in our Pain...
In our Death N in our Livn...
U doing all and elder could do
2 send the message thru...
WAKE UP!!!
N my children know your smiln 4head by heart...
The thick eyebrows and curly head of gray...
The ELDER
daddy watches every sunday...
The ELDER...
tryna change the world from being...
LIKE IT IS

GANJA HAIKUS

Meditation spliff
Lift my heavens ether bound
Groundation runnings

Wadadli herbals
Fresh green sensemilia
Rastafari vibes

Chalice bubbles hot
Churchical hilltop movements
Chant down babylon

Marijuana joint
Ganja makes your mind rebel
Against mankind's 'isms

Smoke sweet kali weed
Poor people medication
Herb heal de nation

GOD?

Who was our God
b4 the white man came...
I mean what was her name?
Did she come from Galilee...
or look like me...
adam's...ADAM?
Apple hell...
mankind FELL...
cuz mankind FAILED!!!
stop lovin...
1 another...
Sista Brodah
...Father Mother
Man 2 beast...
Man 2 earth!
...We hurt 4 gain
N hurt 4 pleasure...
N hurt 4 treasure
In the name of a savior shoved down our throat...
That preachers quote on sunday...
When SUN dey inna center a Kemetic sky...
As RA...
before jesus ever
Come round ya!
Where I-n-I deh...
from creation birth...

As Elegba
CrossRoad sitn...
Watchn missionary step off ships
With poison on their lips...
Whispering contradictions...
Jesus loves U capture!
Jesus loves U brand!
Jesus loves U Goree island!
Jesus loves U ship!
Jesus loves U rape!
Jesus loves U kill!
Jesus loves U jump 2 sharks!
Jesus loves U North America!
Jesus loves U South America!
Jesus loves U Caribbean!
Jesus loves U Suga Cane!
Jesus loves U Tobacco!
Jesus loves U Cotton!
Jesus loves U sharechopn!
Jesus loves U Jim Crow!
Jesus loves U KKK!
Jesus loves U lynchn rope!
Jesus loves U Amadou!
Jesus loves U Sean!
Jesus loves U Trayvon!
Jesus loved U...
away from yourself...
With a bible n a CROSS...
@ the CROSSroad of life...
BcuZ u won't look BLACK...

and remember!!!
Who our GOD was...
B4 the white man's...
came?

1BLOOD

Groundation movements
Sitn with my TRIBE vibn
We share AFRIKA

AN AMERIKKKAN RANT!

Fruit of a barren tree...
Poisoning the partaker with patriotic paranoia...
Eatn regurgitated lies from the beak of a bald eagle...
Raised on propaganda...
Hating flesh of darker hue...
Payn 2 be blessed by priest...
with dirty hands...
N dirty plans...
for little boys seekn "god's" embrace...
Facing cultural extinction...
A bi-product of importing enticed labor...
Who come with visions of betterness...
N go blind...

lookn for the amerikkkan dream...
Of honey N cream...
Altering amerikkka's sense of a census...
With multiplying minorities...
That now make up the majority of amerikkka's population...

EGUN

The smell of plantains fryn...
crustn over sweet
yellow...
orange...
black
Brings U back...
wide feet; flat
against
kitchen floor...
Resettling iron pot
on crimson coals...
With calloused hands that could
hold us tenderly...
and slap
Our bottoms numb
in the same smile...
Anecdotes
dips in leather belts...
Spelled out
in purple whelps...

along our epidermis...
sunshine...
pumpkin fritters
that warmd us
Orange yellow
from the
nside out...
Pour thick tonics
n bush concoctions
n2
reluctant mouths...
Dull hum
of Singer pedal
rockn us 2 sleep...
On UR lap...
nside a cocoon
of love...
N I cry at UR grave
like its still 1978...
And I am still
9 years old...
still upset with myself for not being strong...
enough to catch
U slidn...
from UR
breakfast...
Chair
U Egun now...
carryn prayers
to Obatala's ears...

US (N ODE)

InsiDe US
I am better!
Wet my lips and whistle...
The melody we grind N2 being...
obelisk nside
Ur temple...
Worshipn nside
Ur temple...
Sacred river floods
its banks
and I giVe thanks
2 Obatala...
Place Ebos
2 Oshun under a
full moon...
For more of Ur
honey...
Sipd from ur
Ebony spoon...
Ride pleasure waves
That ebb n flow...
From U 2 me in symbiotic timing...
I ebb U flow...
I ebb U flow...
I ebb U flow...
I ebb U flow...
U flow I flow...

We flow...
2gether in the
original dance...
Indigenous US
Lustn a planet
N2 being...
U melt my angst with ur tropical Sun...
and I give thanks
4 U...
Place Ebos in the rivers of Oshun
2 say...
4 U eYe lust...
and
I am better...
Nside...
US

SUN!

Melanin refill...
Equator calln me
by name...
Akhenaten's revelation...
In the beginning...
B4 the son
of man
Came 2 die...
The SUN
was already N the Afrikan sky...
Photosynthesizing
us
from dust...
Orange glow
on ebony skin...
Alive again...
Sweet sweat drip
from bodies...
wet with anticipatn...
RA's rays...
and RA's haze
of purifying heat...
Walk bare feet
across winter skin...
BluePurpleBlack
West
Afrikan!
again!

BLACKWARDS (4 US)

We stay...
Connectd
by DNA...
Ties 2 a legacy
bastardized and franchised...
By a capitalist state of mind...
Mein Kampf!!!
Against the flood of fascism...
raping the ground beneath my feet...
Teachn me to hate the blood n my veins...
Anglo-saxoning my name...
Be baptized in the name...
I have no name...
I have no home...
I roam the graveyard
of ancestor's bones
strewn across
the planet...
Lookn 4
my D.N.A
The way
Back home...
2 my original chromosomes...

YOU

I
hear
ur
heartbeat
in
mine
feel
mine
in
yours
WOMAN!
F
E
L
L
n2
UR
love
and
let
myself
drown
die
cry
at
the
birth

of
the
man
you
knew
that
I
could
be
B4
eye
ever
saw
him

I GROW (2 BE READ FROM TOP 2 BOTTOM N BOTTOM 2 TOP)

Grow
I
In spite of...
Out of my cocoon
n2 my wings
Pass
negro...
nigger...
my nigga...
African american...
west indian...
Shitn out stereotypes
Facn fears...
Falln over obstacles...
Seeing past
my eyes...
Elegba
points 2wards
2morrow...
N yesterday
Strivn 4 betterness...
I
Grow

RUN A BOAT(COMMUNAL POT)

Disya Ras bring 3 Onyan...
N datde Ras bring
2 Beet...
Bongo bring piece
a Scallion...
de Elda green
peppa dem sweet...
Nato Scrape
Coconut...
Make coconut milk...
I Man wash de
brown rice...
Binghi a mek
couple dumpling...
Dready bring fresh pick spice...
Fari a peel off de pumpkin...
I-nut wata a bubble
ina Yaba...
ova coalpot fiyah...
Man a bring wha
dem can...
N give wha
dem got...
Rasta
a run a
Communal
pot!

DANCE

Clank of
metal spoon...
off
metal pot...
Dripn water drops...
HOT!
In time wid a
Max Roach
snare SNAP...
Ebony fingers
POP!
Hips rock
2 spirit sounds
Heard on
Dogon frequencies...
Boo kack
tu-gu-tu
klack...
Boo kack
tu-gu-tu
KLACK!!!
Put ur back
n2 the grove...
Move!!!
Find U Nside
the beat...
Soul will

summon feet
Without engaging brain...
STOP!!!
thinkn bout it...
LISTEN!!!
and
DANCE!!!

RAIN

Last night
it rained hard N
constant
Spashn off walls N
roofs flowing
thru crevices N
over barriers
Creating a
bouncn
grindn
penetratn
Melody of her N me
We-ing Us-ing
Remembern Caribbean days when
raindrops bouncn off galvanizd roof
played the background melody
2 nights of
Tropical love
making sweat

that fell
N we
Remembered
like raindrops
Wet
On the tip
of my memory
Last night
it rained
Heavy long N hard

YOU2

I watch U sleep at night
Silver moonlight sliver
Highlighting
the Yoruba
in Ur
cheekbones
jawline
bloodline
the line
Ur forehead carves
n2 the space
around U
brings me back thru libations
poured n2 possessed Atlantic
Ocean Screams
rattling chains

Holdn me against splinterd lumber
Unable 2 reach
the throat of
Ur tormentor
I couldn't stop the deconstruction
of our nation
U 4ever patience
Waitn generations
4 me
2 remember
the pact I made
chain 2 my back
2 always have
Ur backative
U made me
want 2
Live again
Dance again
Smile again
Laugh again
Love again
Against odds
that said
I would never
find U
Never
find me
In our corrupted
gene pool
But I pour libations
n2 possessed

Atlantic Ocean
and it brought me back
Here next 2 U
Watchn U sleep
Silver moonlight silver highlighting
the memories
in Ur
cheekbones

BABA

Sat at ur feet
Watchn jewels
fall from you lips
Twinkle in ur eyes
at passing
women's hips
All of it I miss
Old Man
Apple jack askew
Tailor shears
N hand
Coaxing men's wear
From gabardine n polyester
Over Antiguan rum n pipe wata
Over big man
woman talk
that burned my
little boy ears; hot

Diaphragm laugh
that shattered the air around ur head
Ebony Afrikan foot
Finessing Singer pedal
walks along the sea
my hand in yours
Fisherman stories
of ur father
my great grandfather
That always made u smile
n me smile
Cuz ur smile
made me smile...
LAUGH
from the bottom
of my belly
At the joy U brought
2 every day I spent with U
I take them out sometimes
Lay them on the plateaus of my meditations
n LAUGH
ur diaphragm LAUGH
Shattering the air
Around me

LATE 20TH CENTURY SUICIDE NOTE

So I could walk passed/past
a mirror
without lookn away
I killed you!
clampd shut
the umbilical cord
of DNA
between us
needed 2 live
outside your shame
blaming Afrika
4 kissN
Ur skin chocolate Black
Ur nose flared n flat
Ur lips pink n full
Ur nappy hair like wool
"Look! Idi Amin"
made u run from the playground again
my fault u had no friends
truth from a mirror
on the bathroom wall
who's the Blackest of them all
S-curling out
nappy naps
wishn Black skin
lighter...whiter
U had 2 die

so I could live again
Inside my skin again
walkd past/passed
a mirror without
lookn
away

DE OLD LADY'S FUNGI N SALTFISH
(4 MUDDAH VANGI)

(in the Caribbean we call our Mothers n Grandmothers Old Lady,
large O, large L as a sign of endearment and respect...is a West
Afrikan ting ya overstand)

Fungi:
Cornmeal
okra
wata
Love...
A dat de Old Lady say
Wooden spoon
counter clockwise makn
cornmeal okra
wata
one
Love...
Wooden spoond
n2 bowl

n spun
ball a
Fungi
Love...

Saltfish:
3 wata boil off salt

Saltfish si-down; wait
Love...
Skillet stew down
Onion pepper
garlic
Tomato
Wata
Oil
Love...
Add Saltfish
Love...
Set up plate
Fungi ball
Love...
Saltfish stew
Some fu all
Love
Miss de Old Lady
Love

REMEMBA

Rememberd...
on a Mississippi plantation
Felt the lynchd souls of kindred
Emancipation Proclamation out clause
Answerd offer 2 leave n my body
with muddy handprints all over red car
1 day later
Louisiana Voodoo priestess
makes me vomit up christian declaration
N front of Dambala
Then I Rememberd...
old time talk
No mek no body sweep round u foot...
If u eye a jump trouble a come...
Pickney wid long eyelash can see...
jumbi
duppy
spirit
Inherit traits that survive
slave ship n slave whip
Remember...
Moco Jumbi
n Joncunu
what de Obeah Man can do
Rememberd...
Babalawo say Shango's love Kuku(cornmeal n okra)
Remember...

my favorite dish Fungi(cornmeal n okra)
Rememberd...
Fisherman great grandfather's
Admonition in a breakn wave
Rememba Yemaya
Rememba Obatala
Rememba Ifa
Rememba you

THE POET

Iron sharpen Iron
2 an edge
Gleaming in the
white darkness
In spite of...
anyhow...
even though...
Cuz we don't die
we multiply...
Like words
on a page
Like words
for the rage
Instead of raging
against the machine
We go within
2 get out
Of the rat race living
takn time
2 see the prose
in the rose
Thru the thorns
of dreams deferred
heard in the tales of
the Djeli...
the Guewel...
the Gawlo...

the Gnawi..
the Griot ...
the Poet...
Told on street corners
n town centers
n pow wows
n groundations
n dinner tables
n open mics
n social networks
2 any1 willn 2
lend n ear
Lend a soul
hold on 2 the oral history
Passed   from   mouth2ear2mouth2ear2mouth2ear2mouth2ear-
2mouth2ear2mouth2ear2mouth2ear...
2 soul...
until all
our stories
are told!

MY JOY

knew of your coming before you came
dreamt your names
in the midnight sunset of my tomorrow
(5)five ancestors sankofa-d Black
chose my loins 2 travel back
once more down creation's track
children turning father n2 daddy
into purpose; reason for...
reason too...
want betterness
see my reflection in the smile of your eyes
my joy...my joy...my joy
my children...

TALAWA

talawa ghal
dancing past my lustn
woman wafting off da skin she in
tangling dark imagination
in the hairs along her jungle
mango juice juicy
si down unda tree and wait pan dat fu ripe
tonight...
arch in back from shoulders to ass
thighs part...legs bendn at knees
waist dangln in the contemplation
of a warm tongue against the heat of anticipation
perspiration bouncn off skin...
against the walls inside the walls against the walls...
inside
da walls...inside the grip
alterd worship...alter hership
blessns flow
blessns glow
along the curves she cuts n2 the air around her
...slow
honey drips off lips...spilln ova hips
Oshun sweet...
juju strokes recorded in the quivers of her feet
toes point...toes lax.....toes point...toes lax...
fingas nails scrape skin from shoulder
pulln closer

heels dig in deeper...
pulln pleas from deeper
down to primal deeper
speech devolves 2 gruntn deeper
pelvic pulsn deeper
nipples poutn deeper
eyes lockd in trance deeper
Shango dancn deeper
keep her
close enuf to taste the contemplation
of her talawa
talawa: Caribbean patois for thick curvy yummy woman

PAINTER

blood in the paint
paint in the blood
essence of my voodoo
written long hand in hues
that color blues a melancholy-d purple
seekn the balance of complimentary pigments
a yellow dance wid red
that blossoms orange in the morning sun
against the taut of raw canvas
pushd beyond the values black n white
beyond the fight
of warm n cold
cool and light...inside the composition
simultaneous contrast in the colors juxtaposed
a poem for the eyes to hear
the silent explosion of a black line
so convincn in its gesture dat u believe; Black
is talkn hues n talkn blues
loud enuf to taste the solemn hum
of perfect symmetry
meditation in 3 dimensions...on surface flat
surface not
enuf to tell the story singn...
in your head
only dead artist sell paintns
so artist die...
tryna make a livn

selln soul for enuf to get... buy
brushes...paints...and studio space...
blood in the paint
paint in the blood
in my eye...

TOMORROW

old man on donkey
sideway ridn
coax-d along wid strategic
slap from cutlass turnd flat gainst hind parts
carryn a bag fulla yesterdays
in the crocus sack
bouncn gentle gainst the curve of his back
smiles a jagged hello...
to curious bright eye-d boy
face fulla inquisitive
lookn sideways at the sack
...ridn slowly into morrow

REBIRTH

on the day you feel it fall away
...melt into the space between your fingers
random silhouette of yesterdays
fade in2 the grayn dance of memories...
let go...
allow the purge to take...
the change to make
you uncomfortable...restless
wid only de wings blossom-n inside
2 keep the fragile shell holdn soul
from plummetn to rocks below...
trust the wind
tis' the same breeze that took the words
ancestors scream-d from hangn trees...
!spirits!
releas-d from the sugarcane cottonfield tobacco crop
bondage of european economies...
same breeze that took the ebo's
of Babalawos to Oludumare for the protection of stolen blood
Ase O!!!
same breeze
that blew through the kingdoms invent-n writn and architecture
language and culture...Ase O!!!
and up the Nile and down the Congo
across the Euphrates
into the Mississippi
same breeze...Ase O!!!

same breeze that blew through the midwife's hut
in the beginning...Ase O!!!
when the planet gave birth to earth/womb/man
same breeze...Ase O!!!
same breeze...Ase O!!!
same breeze...Ase O!!!
blowing you into the tradewinds of UR destiny
on wings growing slowly
from the hunger of your soul
...just let go!!!
Ase O!!!

LAUGH

laugh in the swallow of a million pains
laugh...in spite of...
we laugh...we who live
on the cross hairs of ur fears
spook burn-n down the door
to your peace of mind...
laugh-n
jigaboo with a watermelon slice
you fry chicken-d into a mouthful a stereotypes
laugh-n
shot after...lynch-d...stop-d and frisk-d into
a file in an office at the local babylon station
channel-n the rage inside the cage
laugh-n
in spite of...even though

still finds glee in see-n my newborn's chocolate face
smil-n up at me
watch-n 'em grow each day
laugh-n
in spite of the odds
growing into everything the stereotypes aint
Black on both sides...Black inside out...
Black dogma com-n out of mouth
laugh-n
kujichagulia in the face of ur opinion
of my right to walk creation
with the peacock in my chin at 45 degrees
laugh-n
joy intact
happy to be Black
laugh-n
in spite of...even though...
I still smile...
still find laughter in the journey
laugh!!!

BLACK WOMAN

She shines orange yellow
like a tomorrow sun
bright with possibilities
female by choice
voice of a million mouths
wid shoulders to hold up a nation of men
pussing at the core
whores to a dick-tionary definition
stuck in the reflection of a phallic philosophy
symbol of a shallow existence...
letn her down too often
coffins fill-d wid too many
baby imma do bettas...
she perseveres; carries load on
shoulders numb
thru enuf european cum to wipe a DNA away
and she endures
mulatto pickney strapd to a hip
quadroon strapd to de other
octoroon against her back
all wailn Mother...
Waitn for the blue eyes
occupyn her breast
to feed so they can suckle too...
she female by choice
voice stifled by tradition
fights thru the contradiction
of men who create nations

GRANDFADAH

adolescent joys of boundless running
naked feet behind naked byci-kle rim...
peesa ben wiyah steer-n
flying kite cross tumbln cobalt sky
high pantopa mango tree
belchn belly fulla mango
belchn laughn fits of mango juice on school shirt
that guarantees ringn ears from tender cuff
gainst..."bouye you head too frign hard!"
findn...
manhood in a haze of calypso fever
grindn gainst the tropical curves of a island ghal
learning...
the safety of a woman's vagina
in the heat of a 3rd world light
with the breeze of a 3rd world night
blowing slow against the nakedness of the moment
tradn too many lies for too many thighs
partd in submission to a mouthful of sugar words
pourd down ear canal into captive heart
pulld out of 5 vaginas too slow...10 times
leavn 3 boys n 7 girls
fu me granny ge he 1 a de boy and 3 a de ghal
aunty jennifer the first left the planet at 6 months old
victim of a guinep seed
my mother their redemption came 6 months later...
he lov-d her tremendously
they shar-d farts and belly laughs and sense of humor

and whistl-n and art and dark mahogany skin
I came 18 yrs and 9 months later
first grand pickney...I lov-d him tremendously
he step-d in when my father step-d off
became my daddy
taught me bout running nak-d feet
bhind nak-d byci-kle rim steer-d wid ben wiyah
flyn kite cross tumbl-n cobalt sky
talk mommy out of ass whip-n deserv-d
wid "ghal a one bouye he be...lef he."
whistl-n to the music of a woman hips
walk-n pass the tailor shop...
miss the presence of his 6-5 frame
wedg-d behind the singer creat-n art in cloth
the treble of his baritone...
"bouye...come down outta dey mango tree
and gwarn go buy de tread gemme!"
miss the blue "big man" talks bout blue women
and the proclamations of his legendary day...
"since me wake dis marning a 6 a dem me slay!"
miss the belly laughs and brassy farts
miss the twinkl-n eyes and the lov-n heart
miss...
my Baba

SUGAR

I come from suga cane people
who cut cane so de white people
inna europe coulda sweeten dem tea
cutlass and ducketts wata boots
sun up to sun gone sweatn suga wata...
drinkn suga wata...

fiber from crocus bag haffu strain outta
dutty brown suga dem save fu poor people
table fulla white people throw way...
tun salt cod inna stew down saltfish
overripe banana n pumpkin tun fritters
ha dem a falla dem nose outta dem big house
down to wey allwe dey wid allwe coalpot
fulla charcoal and ashes
a mek sumting outta de nutn dem ge allwe
a survive inna shoot hard labor...
a get likkle and nutn fu do everyting
til every stalk a cane gone a mill

so when u see me a nyaam
cane; sweet with the labor of Eguns gone
mouth fulla sweat n perseverance
suckd from stalk...
grown in soil...
rich with the blood of their tears
know that I live in the glow of their hope

call their names in the shadows of the remnants
of those suga mills
still dotn the landscape today
decayn odes to the blood sacrifice
of suga cane people
who cut cane
so de white people
inna europe coulda sweeten dem tea

("shoot hard labor" is a Caribbean term for sharecropping)

HERBS

inna one ibration
unda me sensi...
binghi checkn out de scene...
sight up higha highs
inside the twirl of ishen floatn
up into the ether
flash knotty through the sky and trod creation
greetn all vibrations wid love n 1ness
stressless...
hill top dwelln
bubbln ital pot a ital stew
from I cultivation of greens and herbs
blaze chalwa blend up
nice wid ibacco and tampi; nutmeg screen in place...
chase the crazy bald heads out de space
free up heavens

tek off tam...free up Knotty and
pass de kuchi inna rotation
til wata start bubble...
and everybody irie
unda dem sensi
goat skin keti cracks the silence
wid Dogon sound waves older than invention
when heartbeat echoing inside chest
inside soul...easy skankn...takn it easy...takn it slow
letn go
slow enuf to hear mother nature's voice in the blowing breeze
gainst ganja leaves bloomn into buds
of love

NATIVE TONGUE

funji saltfish and fat
nuthing sweeta than dat
if you want um fu come likkle sweeter
slap de choba pan top...
34 years on foreign soil...toiln away
trying to find my voice in a "fit in or get out" world
endure banana boat teasing
hidn native tongue to get along
bend under the wave of hegemonic bias
by people wid skin like the one i'm in
pissd off thinkn I want their place
on the american totem pole of class
last; below a century of immigrants

who came with the right/white skin
and got ellis islanded in...
each takn the stairwell of black backs
up to their place in the statue of liberty
I swallow words and ride along...
head down; mother tongue tuckd away
avoidn confrontation
african american by proxy
talkn fluent yankee...relegatn native mouth
to home and private moments
til moments grow in distance
til memories grow in distance
til native tongue grows distant into ancient memory
banished to special occasions when family comes
or if you go to Brooklyn...
Land of a thousand immigrants
the flood of native tongues rush your senses
pluck your brain away from fitn in long enuf
to drown in the embrace of culture...
long enuf to remember wey you come from
and wha you ado ya?
the yankee words ceases...run out...stop...dry up
nothing comes...
vomit up a mouthful of spoken words to become a poet
nothing comes...
words return in a flood of patois
voice inside says...when you nar write de words and dem
how you just tink dem...
muse comes back dress in a calypso of tropical
words bright and burstn with life...
I stay out of the way n let dem flow

with a humble Ase O...
to Eguns who took pleas
to Obatala for me.

Fungi: Caribbean dish made from cornmeal n okra.

Fat: a "gravy" made with cookn oil, tomato paste n onions, saltfish is stewd down in it

Choba: eggplant spinach n okra mixd together n seasond wid black pepper n butter

Yankee: talking and acting american the verb is yanking

BLUEST EYE

bluest eyes
she spent all her time wishn
for a different her
something that wouldnt say
Africa so loud...
wouldnt have her hearing...
"you're pretty for a dark skin sista" so often
would'nt have her bringn every dolla
to the korean man selling black hair products
at the corner store down the block
who goes out of his way
to take her money
widout touchn the rumors of her flesh...
wearing dead hair over her crown
of original woman
running away from her legend
already carved into the pillars of history
so she spends 2 hours each risn of the sun
powdern "lighter skin in a can"
over the original ebony of her bloodline
covering the pride of nation buildn
queen mothers
who suckld a planet into being
when the abundance of melanin in her skin
was the only thing keepn
the sun at bay...
made to walk with chin aloft...

neck reachn...
shoulders squared against the air
around her...
holdn the gaze of kings
before europe calld them chiefs
and teef off alla allwe sense a self
n put allwe culture pan museum shelf
dead; to a people; dead
to the life before slavery
b4 inferiority complex had them measuring
success with european measuring sticks
had them worshipn the ego trips
of men pretendn to be gods
pretendn to be civilized...pretendn to be
the men...
that we pretend to be everyday
with our bleachn cream
and our I got a receipt so it's mine
and our I got indian in my family
and our perms
and our conks...and our lyes...
and our bluest eyes

MOMMY (HAPPY BIRTHDAY)

the first time I saw Africa
she was lookn down into my eyes
with the hope and anxiety of a "girl mother"
19 and in trouble with my grandmother
19 and in love with my wayward father
19 and alone wid a baby lookn up into her face
and we grew together
mother son friend...softening the
sting of my father's absence
my sista nicky was their peace pact
brought our family back together
til daddy was gone again
and we grew together
mother son daughter friends
softening the sting of my father's absence
she became our everything
mother father
teacher protector
savior executioner
"bouye me go run off and jump inna you chest"
was enuf of a threat for me to never
seek dat repercussion
just she and us sojourned to merrica
lookn for our tomorrow
she put batteries in boxes to pay for our lives
for wages that amountd to 3.75
an hour 7 days a week

she left the stress at work
and brought home smiles...so we never knew
how much her feet hurt...
how much her back hurt
how much she stretchd the little she got
to give us all we needed
and when Tarik came she filld in for his father too
doing all that she could do
and we grew together
mother daughter sons friends
guiding all of us to adulthood
on her strength of will
on her strength of character
on the strength of an African woman
inventing tomorrows
the first time I saw Africa
she was lookn down into my eyes
with the smile of a Serengeti sun
I calld her Mommy

ANTIGUAN; ANTIGUAN

wake up like dis
dis morning
feeling Antiguan; Antiguan(if a word is repeated, the 2nd time its
a punctuation)
more than usual...
more than go supermarket
go buy force ripe mango
more than Jamaican pattie
from unda heatn lamp
at the Spanish bodega
down the block
more than a big spliff a head food usual...
dis marning me feel like me warn go
a me yard 2rarted
tell merrica hold yo mudah skunt
and go bout me business...cha!!!
mek one kite outta de immigrant tribulations
stick um down wid clamancherry/turkleberry...
and fly way
strip off dis too long winter
stand up naked in de Caribbean sea
and mek Yemeya baptize me; again
like before when likkle sea wata
and piece a allas(aloe)
coulda cure everything; anything...every time; anytime
remember tropical me
great grandson of a fisherman

swallow likkle sea wata
listen til the waves becomes my Baba's laugh
echoing off the colbalt sky
pull trade wind breezes into my lungs
til they fill and brim over
purple; like the stain of a beach grape
gainst the purple black skin
of an island boy
running along the pink sand
who woke up dis morning
feeln Antiguan Antiguan

BLACK!

Black on both side
Black inside out
Black comn out of mouth
Black...through the connotation...
Black...and the designation
Black with a power fist for the stop and frisk
Black inside the hail of bullets; livn through it...
black devils food cake...
black mail...
black sheep...
black listed...
black hearted...bad guys wear
black always black...
black clothes...
black hat...

Black cat
Black kat in
Black leather and
Black afro
Black Panther
Black love
Black Man
Black Woman
Black Child
Black Revolution(change)
Black on both sides
Black inside out
Black comn out of mouth
BLACK!

SOBUKWE

Black Obelisk...
tall against the Azanian sky
sure as the click of a Xhosa tongue
legacy un-corrupted in the winds of reconciliation
conceding too much for peace
land is still the basis of all opportunity
still lacking to the Blacks that walk the land
homeless at home
on the ground raped by rhodes n debeers
(they don't deserve capital letters)
for more years than make sense
in a world that covets the diamonds n gold of Afrika's soul
sold for too cheap
exported for too cheap
and bought back for too much
as western/eastern imports
made in the usa made in china
made to keep a continent discontent
and divided into galvanize townships
franchised at election time
walkn talkn placard
for a bag of rice
for a bag of promises
for another politrickan's 2step
round your sense of common sense
1 step forward 2 steps back
into worrying more bout what white people want

than what Black people need
greedy to a fault
progress sacrificed for personal gain...again...
at the people lost
in the truths n rights commission
with no right to see the justice of truth
beyond fork tongued apologies
that stink of apartheid predilections
in modern day Capetown
where privileged cracker woman in afrikaan's skin
walk round Black Caribbean poet
in local drug store like he aint there...
next door to the Mandela rhodes hotel
where all is well
for the haves
and the people still have not
and the winds screams Mayibuye
swirln round
the Black Obelisk
tall against the Azanian sky

SARKI BAARTMAN

All the shit the white woman do
to look like you
tryn to recapture the white man's eye
pull him back from tabooing Afrika
lustn after the mystery of your chocolate flesh
wanting to sample
your ample-ness
the honey of your breast
the rounding of your ass
the curving of your hips
the fullness of your lips
your perfect nakedness
stuck in their display case
petri dish dissections
while their women yearn your silhouette
in their 18th century skirt support
paniers and bouffants
tied round hips
bums, rumps and cul
lied round hips
stuff under frocks
to bring back the eyes of men
lustn for Afrika again
and I meet you in Kimberley
in Upington...
in Springbuk...
in Alexandra...

in Soweto...
in Capetown...
in JoBurg...
in Leliefontein...
resurrected in your daughters hips
roundn into perfect ass...perfect melody
walkn down the street
passing curve-less white women
still smiln at your beauty
with jealous botox lips
tryn to recapture the white man's eyes
pull him back from his taboo
the shit white woman do
to look like you

MAYIBUYE

in a flood of tears
crestn up 500 years
triggered by the sharing of a poem
that came to my pen after 3 days of listening
3 days of lustn at the music in the words
heard long before the caveman came
familiar on the tip of mother tongue
trapd inside the english in my head
trapd behind the bible verses
cursed to hold the legacy of Ham
doomd to walk the land of my captors
cross seven generations
til Afrika was just an ancient meditation
and the words slip thru my fingers
like sweet water

in a flood of tears
crestn up 500 years
I felt the welcome home
circle of elders warms my trembling flesh
elder pulls me to his chest
wipes tears from my face
to his face inside the embrace
kisses wrapped in hugs wrapped in kisses
welcome home Sun...
we never forgot u Sun...

we love you Sun...
Mayibuye-bring it back
lifts the burden from my back...
Mayibuye bring it...
back to feeln completely
whole...
replenishd my tortured soul...

in a room filld with tears
crestn up 500 years

RASTA DEY A AFRIKA (4 THE IDREN IN SPRINGBUK SA)

Rasta dey a Afrika
foundation sound
chanting down
babylon shitstem
babylon miss dem growing thru the cracks
along apartheid's back
walkn naked foot
into a tomorrow fulla possibilities

Rasta dey a Afrika
beatn thundabolt outta kheti drum
Natty skankn
Binghi hopn
chantn down babylon shitstem
Babylon miss dem growing thru the cracks
Along apartheid's back
naked foot gainst naked earth
creation birth
chantn equal rights and justice

Rasta dey a Afrika
ganja smokn
meditation irie
herbal congregation
1ness in the sacrament of ishen
chillum fiyah hot

seeing thru the babylon illusions
bloodline comn from creation
chantn down Babylon shitstem
Babylon miss dem
Growing thru the cracks
along apartheid's back

Rasta dey a Afrika
roaming home
the lion Zion
livn in the livity of His Majesty
Haile Selassie
whether Bobo Wrap up
or Nyabinghi
12 Tribes
or Knotty Dread
chantn Rastafari!

Rasta dey a Afrika
chantn love and 1ness
walkn naked feet
thru foundation
spreading earth vibes
and people rhythms
Rasta dey a Afrika

MOUNTAIN IBRATION(RASTA WORD FOR MEDITATION)

morning mountaintop ibration
diamond voices in the wind
truth as clear as a new sky
boundless cumulus clouds drift
soundless cept the singn in my ear
400 years and its the same philosophy
400 years and the people still cant be free
walkn round wid the surname of the muthafucka
who fuck ur motherland-less
nameless spiritless cultureless
and filld the void with
2nd class schizophrenic existence
internal wars that manifest external self-hate
indoctrinated people
fighting to be equals wid invadn
blood raiders who steal the land
and kill the man...
who rape the land
and rape the woman...
birthn stereotypes whose lives
begin and end on the words of white men

sip spliff...
inhale Afrikan morning
send prayers and contemplation
to Eguns in meditation

givn thanks in benediction
for protection
gainst a beast who wants my flesh
in the center of the bullseye
in the tangle of the crosshairs
in the township of a beast
who wants my flesh...

sip spliff
exhale stress and botheration
in my Rastaman ibration
in this morning time vibration
givn thanks for Jah's creation

AFRIKA(5 HAIKU)

neon cobalt sky
cotton candy clouds float by
I inhale and drift

soil of my bloodline
endure goree island blues
sold soul back to soil

waterfalls blooms rainbow
baboon feeding young at dawn
Azania morning

Swaziland Ganja
sipd from cup on mountaintop
and I'm already high

black foot on red dirt
in the land of my birth-right
I inhale and drift

THE RAISN OF A PIG (4 WALTER SCOTT)

in the shadow
of an oak tree hauntd by Mississippi
in a congregation of unholy men
bent on spilln blood
in carnal sacrifice
that reek of medieval ritual
hiding participation behind white sheets
that cover dark hearts
dark as the forsaken conscience
planted in the darkness of jim crow
burning crucifixion in feathers and tar
scorched into the hearts of suckling babes
with hate as hot as purgatory
nurtured on the convictions of a nation
for the people by the people...
with white skin and white privilege
tortured by the "what if" of righteous vengeance
murder as a sedative to feed the ghost
of memories that come when they feel
and leave when they feel...
sipn sarsaparilla on daddy's shoulder
in the shadow of that oak's swingn rope
learning right and wrong
learning white and black
learn to tie a lynching knot
learn to shoot a lynching shot...
in the shadow of that oak tree

justifications wrapd
in machinations of monster
black men that rape the blue-eyed blondness
of white womanhood
perpetually Bigger Thomas
perpetual boogie man
in the cathedral of whiteness
to be feared at all cost
protect the women n children
white...
protect the women and children
white...
protect the...
white women and children
in their Rapunzel tower of goodness
hidn participation
behind blue walls
of silence...

4 MANGO HAIKU

my mango woman
juicy from the center out
sticky on my chin

ripened on the vine
sunshine bouncing off ur skin
can't wait to eat you

peel you with my teeth
one slow mouthful at a time
til nothing no left

sometimes one mango
aint enough to quench the want
quell the taste for you

DAT POEM

when the words...
dont come
and the music dances...
just outside the reach of your ears
and the pen drags slow
across the page
straining phrases...
chokn cliches from the keys
torturing metaphors and similes
into clumsy chunky lines
that stumble from ur lips
and land in a thud
against the papyrus
forever utter...
STOP!!!
put down the pen
walk away from keyboard
and leave the poem
alone...

MUDAH TONGUE

this shit hurts!
listening to a tongue
dragd from my mouth
in the belly of a slave ship
trapped in the memory of remembering
the melody...
the syntax...
the cadence...
the phonetic structure...
the dance of words...
on the tip of my tongue
teasing my recollection
evading my overstanding the words
slipn thru my fingers
like sweet wet water...
gone before I can sip its substance...
quench the thirst
burning down my need
to belong
in the land
of my blood

THE POVERTY OF HOPE

they drag bags
thru the streets of JoBurg
recycln the city
stuck in a circle of poverty
smile thru the struggle for dignity
the smiles of pity
from faces that avoid their eyes
and avoid their truth
the paycheck to paycheck thin line
separatn class systems

honkn horns...
swerving around dem
pushn their existence
thru the streets of New York
recycln the city
begn for a means
one penny at a time playn on the pity
of people livn one paycheck away
from their reality

dragn their baggage behind them
wrapd in the shiny trapns
of "successful"
and the 30 day cycle
of bills and livn

bills and livn...to pay
bills and livn...
to pay...
bills...

DAY DREAMN

smell of fresh cut grass
brings days of boyhood tumbles
down memory lane

MIRROR IMAGE

truth from a mirror
on the wall of ur conscience
you do not like the things you see
they rub wrong gainst the western sense of self
u sip intravenously...
life line...main lining western civilization
in lines drawn across a continent
of people already divided by idiosyncrasies
exploited by pink skin thieves
that take souls and gold
and leave dividn lines
across a continent of people
already divided by exploited idiosyncrasies
of Bloods against Crips
Zulu against Xhosa
black american against black Caribbean
Santa Dominican gainst Haitian
black South African gainst black Zimbabwean
black fist bounce off black face
black foot gainst black ribs
black hand holds black gun
shoots black bullet thru black flesh
leaves black mother in black dress
shakn black fist into a black sky
askn why...
black skin gainst black skin
red blood on black asphalt

burnt permanently into the streets of Durban
in the name of xenophobia
fightn over a space
a place
in a world created by pink skin thieves
who take souls n gold
and leave dividn lines
across a people
already divided
against
themselves

ISHEN

from a chillum pipe
sip mellow meditations
that sprinkle moonlight purple
and lift in Izes(praises)
n2 the yellow ether

from a big head spliff
sip mellow ibrations
that swirls into the night
on Nyabinghi chants
n2 the ital ether

from a chalice cup
sip Afrikan groundation
that clap into the silence night
on kheti drum vibrations
n2 the risn ether

AMERIKKKA

another black man
got killed by the cops today
...pass the ketchup

2 LIKKLE WHITE BOY

Two likkle white boy get kill today
shot down inna de street
wrong place wrong time
wrong Black Man dem find...
cause dem look dangerous
and me no trust
dem...look to much
lakka dem grandpupa convictions...
look lakka dem woulda
do wat dem alway do
so allwe shot dem dead
fore dem shot allwe fus
fu dem mumma must...
put on black dress
make outta stressn
if dem pickney a come home tonite
fu dem mumma can
feel likkle a de blight
dat allwe mumma feel every night...
a time fu dem hold fu dem belly too
bawl murder blue
bawl blue wall murder blues
ca' two likkle white boy
get shot down tonite
ca' allwe ready fu fight
fu allwe rights!
time dem mumma
hold dem belly and cry

and wonda why
so much likkle
white boy
a die?

MOSADI WA NTLHA MO LEFATSHENG

purple blue black woman
in the morning of my brightest day
sunshine ricochet
against the angle of ur jawline
trace the line ur hips make
in the air around them
back to that first star kiss
when God made woman in her image
and saw that she would
suckle a planet into being

purple blue black woman
source of the water flowing
from the center of creation
into ancient rivers
magic in the embryonic cradle of life
screaming ancient incantation
to the ritual of birth
at the risn of the Sun
of man's first footsteps
on the ground that first bore seeds

purple blue black woman
standn tall against the tapestry of tomorrow
ancient futuristic lover
of my wild imaginations
locked inside the rhythm of ur loving
dance a thousand dances
a thousand years as one
each time i hold your hand

(Mosadi wa ntlha mo lefatsheng is a Setwana phrase it means first woman on the planet)

MAGIC VAGINA

in the blink of a forth night
in the glow of a tangerine moon
she lay in a bed of contemplation
conjuring spells that corrupt
the lust of mortal men...
magic vagina...Oshun waters
drip virgin honey
by the tongue full
sticky stuck sticky fuck(n)
honey comb that grabs
and releases...
grabs and releases...
in a heatd throb
as old as the drum
cum in time wid da beat

of hand gainst taut skin
slap original melody
that arches spine and swivels hips
in original dance...
the grind
that birth mankind

AFRIKAN

Black foot on red dirt
under cobalt sky
in the embrace of a motherland
at the foot of an elder
learning about my yesterdays
that even generations removed
...i feel in the back of my memory now
there...where the remnants of my psyche
took refuge in the days of genocide
when the backra came
wid their bloody meditations

Black backs
on splinterd white spruce
chained in supermarket soup can rows
of products for retail
in the stomach of 18th century
euro-merican triangle atlantic capitalism
that even generations removed
still linger in the remnants of my psyche
there...in the back of my recollections
when the backra came
with their bloody meditations

Black boy
on black asphalt
under a troubled sky

dead as Martin King's dreams
of an equal america
born on the cross hairs 1998
died on the cross hairs 2015
almost 18 years into a sentence
of life as public enemy number one
still clinging to the remnants of my psyche
there in the back of my memory
in the backra's world
trapd in their bloody meditations
for Emmett Tilling a white girl

Black People
gather in village square
under a new sky
ancestor's cries ringing in their ears
remember the days...
before the
backra came
before they took our names
and gave us theirs
with their bloody meditations
Black foot on red dirt
under cobalt sky
in the embrace of a mother land
before the backra came

(backra is Caribbean patois for white people we gave them the
name becuz in our sun their white skin especially the back would
get burnt and raw...back raw)

RIOT!!!

pushed people
pushed past the precipice
will eventually
push back

RIOT2!!!

much maligned
into a lack of choices
at the mercy of ur conqueror...
policed by gestapo in blue...
impulse driven need to be heard
and be seen
boiln in the bloody waters
of too many years of begn
and pleadn for the right
to exist...to flourish and grow
unencumbered by a mindset
set in the corner stone
of america's psyche

melting pot bubbles
over into red hot rage
against the machine that
pulls the strings of captured people
forced to live inside the confines
of a history book of stereotypes

destroying the environment
destroying them
with overpriced merchants
who come to exploit the spending habits
of perpetual consumers
who consume too much fructose

sodium & saturated fats
and police who skip the target range
for the hood
and the thrill of killn three 5ths of a man
and a news media that chooses
sensationalism over truth
shock over substance
from talkn heads who stand in front of every story
so you can see them first

"this morning I woke up in a curfew
ohhh lawd I was a prisoner too
could not recognize the faces standing over me
they were all dress in uniforms of brutality"
-Marley

RIOT3!!!

give me liberty
or give me ur death
cuz me a plan fu fight to me last breath
and before I'd be a slave
I'd skip over your grave
and go home to my people and be free
swing low sweet chariot
running with Harriet
thru this concrete jungle life
where the livn is hardest
and police kill at will
well I've run out of cheeks
to turn...so burn baby burn
and we don't need no water
let this muthafucka burn!!!

RIOT4!!!

implosion in red white n blue
all over you...
...your sense of safety!

in the land of the free
to be everything
...but black
and tired of the
hoping...
generations gone
carried like magic talisman
tucked into the satin lining
of their everyday coffins
begn at the door
of a house
they built...

in the land of the free?

RIOT5

revenge is a muthafucka!

wondering
when...
and if...
or will I...
do the things
you did to me...
back to you
...because you know
that's what you'd do
and what you been doing
for centuries...
dragn your bloody culture
cross continents
leavn graves in your path
leavn slaves...
who used to be men
in your path...
guardn the doors of your kingdom
with their lives
watchn the shadows
for spooks
who sat at
your door

HANDS

I overstand the loss of innocent life
gone in a forgotn breeze of history; too soon
too many things never got to do...
the coo of a newborn
rustle of a breeze thru summer leaves
perfection of a grandmother's hug
a mother's smile
feel of cool water gainst thirsty throat
midday sun along skin
pleasure in a lover's groan
pain inside a mourner's moan
hands thrown...
into sky scream why...
hands helping wounded...
hands begging to be plucked from the carnage
hands clinched in dispair
hands clutched in fear
hands clasped in prayer
and I would pray for you belgium
but I aint got no fuckn hands

SUSPICIOUS

guarded; as a consequence of our reality
Interactions framed by blood and exploitation
nation buildn with natural resources
taken with a gun and a bible
and a smile and a promise
and a foot gainst the door of my progress
and...
I Dont trust u

LIGHT! (4 ITSREALIGHT)

libation poured gainst dirt 4 you;
Itsrealight...Ase
fore I begin...Ase O!
Sista Poet dagger mouth Woman
crystal ball eyes lookn past your years
a million tears a million times
a million whys
brilliant troubled soul sometimes
worn on sleeve sometimes
left on stage with honesty too loud to ignore, every time...
hummingbird throat Woman
beatbox melody in four part harmony
4ever dancing in my ear
Ase O!

2MORROW CHILDREN

we the children of tomorrow
promise of a people
hoping gainst colonial sentiments
praying into foreign skies
juju dancing keti drumming
juju dancing keti drumming
keti drumming juju dancing
holding one another thru the darkness
loving one another thru the pain
knowing that the journey back to Africa
would never come again
inside that stolen flesh
so far away from home
lamentation in the shit-uation
procreation gainst abject annihilation
in the divination of a prayer
into foreign skies
for the children of tomorrow

AMERICANT

post racial america?
post racial?
post america?
pre america?
B.C...ie...before caucasians came in ships
racing to be the empire on top the hill
racism as a means to an end
with a bloody bible and a righteous bullet
in the name of jesus and white supremacy
and founding fathers
who died for the sins their sons and daughters
will commit in defense of their legacy
of take and destroy
rape and destroy
destroy and destroy
til all that is left is the naked truth
of your white friend at work
who will vote for donald trump
becuz he reminds her of a time
when apple pie
still tasted like apple pie...

BLACK MUSIC

blacker than a white rapper
and his album of the year
so don't tryda elvis presley me with no shit
bout eminem being the baddest
you stan getz-ing me
get the pat boone outta here...
go kenny g that shit to someone who aint never heard
Trane's horn speak in parables
hello...hello...
adele wouldn't know what the hell to do
if Gladys gave her a note to hold
til she got to Georgia on a midnight train
thru the chittling circuit
eric claptoning rolling stoning our blues
into white ears
that would rather hear
Black music
coming outta
white mouths

BLOOD

blood; we no dey forget oooo
even if u tek um...
trek um cross ocean...
cross arabian sand
man woman and child
leavn cemeteries in ur wake o
we go still know
we go still memba Mamma Afrika!
we go bend una english
bend una french
bend una spanish
til you can't hear um again
we go hide we Juju inside u bible
and Voodoo u communion
dance djembe rhythms into u foreign soil
til u think the Watusi is a fox trot
left foot here right foot there
we go mek u say banjo n okra
ducuna n fungi
we no dey forget um
Can't forget um...
the Blood

AFRIKA360

face to the sun
inhaling the salt of the sea
remembering the memories
haunted holy waters
lapping gainst shin bone
chains melt into oceans
flowing backwards...flowing homewards
counter triangle counter intelligence
to remember the me I was
before the western brainwash
drowned my memory
of where the flat of my foot bottom
last touched African soil
face to the sun
inhaling the salt of the sea
remembering ME!

COLO-MENTALITY

bad hair on a bad hair day
toothless comb lost too many tug of wars
peasy head pickanagar* bouye
light skin ambi ambitions
cant dream past slavery
DNA denial at the crossroad with Elegba in ur ear
laughn at ur predicament
bent on running from the comfort of ur flesh
barkn jesus pavlov's dog
see spot run...
see spot sit...
see spot answer to his name
see spot worship pavlov's God/doG
"bark...bark"...good boy spot
cat o nine stuck in throat
magazine movie screen mirror
lied to you again...
you still dont look like dem

*pickanagar=children

BORROWED ENGLISH

whamek fu allwe talkn ahno language yet
no bada forget unu never teach we u tongue
we hear unu tongue
and learn um...
we learnt that shit lissning to y'all
talkn y'all ofay talk...
and we dey mix um wid we tongue you dey beat outta we head o
yeah maufucka dont be ackn like you kaint hear
why our shit aint language yet
you no dey remember how you come to hear your oyibo tongue
ahno latin ee come from?
a cause a arwe...
a da mek ee a tek unu so long
fe recognize um...
we dey tek una tongue
and change um o...
we took all that shit you crackers say
and rock it our way
we tek way unu tongue
and do wha we wan wid um
arwe tek allyou rassclart tongue
and change um

DEATH 2 THE WHITE ART WORLD

(an ode 2 Jean Michel Basquiat...rest very well my brodah...dey
still dont realize u was talkn bout dem in all ur shit)

Basquiat as a novelty
status symbol to a gaggle of rich muthafuckas
famous collectors signing autographs
on original work bought cheap from artist
hoping to make it big
bent at the knee for a show in new york
at a gallery who makes you help them steal your shit
and suffern and smiln cuz ur in the circle now
and wine and cheese and art for art sake
by artist who pander to the status quo
to go to europe and be the next...
dead ass Basquiat sold for 4 million
to a rich rapper buying stock in white culture
overlooking Norman Lewis cuz white people
aint say he was great yet...
waiting in line like good niggas to be recognized
by a white art world forever flirting with
the erotic nature of Blackness
telln us what greatness looks like
what movement is...
what "Modern Art" looks like
so we can drink it intravenous
and wait in lines to see what you tell us is good
at the latest art basel

where you can buy gold plated shit
for two hundred thousand dollars
in the name of art!

WATER

water; e no get enemy
ano wata fault politrickans think lakka dis
pissing on equal rights...
people's right...
to drink...and bathe...
and cook dey food
reaction slow drips a familiar rhythm of
a no be me...
me no care...
we have clear wata out here...
away from urban blight...
where people have to fight to quench
their thirst for equal rights
in a "1st world" nation...
waiting in a line for water ration
dripn dropn...dripn dropn
dripn dropn...dripn dropn...
dirty Detroit water

SOUR LEMONS

In a world where everyone sips the lemonade
while skipn past the woes of the planet...
beyon-sanity
kardasianed into history's shallowest epoch
plugged into a virtual reality
lived by celebrities' slaves to the slave master's rhythm
robots in formation
with a bag fulla hotsauce
and a mouth
fulla lemonade

G.O.A.T

like a right hook no one saw
jaw electrified...
wired to the truth
in your face...like it or not
bomaye bomaye bomaye
Ali kill their lies!!!
Ali open eyes!!!
Ali kill their lies!!!
Ali open eyes!!!
gave them back their clay
and their western manhood mold
pretty, black, butterfly flying past their hold/hole

past their boxed in point of view
integrity intact in spite of...
embracing ur blackness in spite of...
in the face of...
a shit-stem that wanted u to Joe Louis ur Jack Jackson
in a flurry of footwork
float like a butterfly
in a flurry of footwork
sting like a bee
in a flurry of footwork...
ALI!!!

FU YOU TONGUE HEAVY LAKKA 56

in my ear she whisperd
you tongue heavy like 56
you ha plenty fu fix
and plenty fu say
heavy like 56
noboda throw um wey
heavy like 56
put you mouth pan dem
when dem lie
hold dem to task...
if dem try...
too much ah allwe done dead
tongue chop outta allwe head
talkn truth into the center
of their storm
recite it like a psalms...
tell our story
in the memory of the djeli the jali
the guewel the gawlo...
the tory bringa and de singa...
tell the stories...in my ear she whisperd
you tongue heavy like 56
you ha plenty fu say
heavy like 56
noboda throw um wey

Putting this book together gave me a wonderful opportunity to reflect back on twenty-seven years of writing poetry. Tis a pretty irie view from here, I still remember the first piece writing in an Iowa jail cell. The first time performing a piece in front of the Black Student Union at S.C.S.U; the first time I stepped on stage at the world famous Brooklyn Moon Café; the first time slamming with the Connecticut poetry team at the nationals in Rhode Island. They were all important points on my journey as a writer.

Each stage fed and informed the next and continues to inspire my exploration into the craft of writing. As a multi-disciplined artist, writing has become another of the tools I use to tell the story.

"Heavy lakka 56" is my first attempt at reflection, the poetry has absolutely evolved, but most importantly for me is the role the exploration of the craft played in that growth.

There is a natural chronology to the work, but that was as far as I went when it came to grouping the pieces into to any type of categories (love, social etc). I love to read poetry and for me the spontaneity is what I'm drawn to most often.

Peace n 1ness
Iyaba